To the Reader . . .

"World Cities" focuses on cities as a way to learn about the major civilizations of the world. Each civilization has at its roots the life of one or more cities. Learning about life in the great cities is essential to understanding the past and present of the world and its people.

People live in cities for many reasons. For one thing, they value what cities can offer them culturally. Culture thrives in all cities. It is expressed in visual arts, music, and ethnic celebrations. In fact, a city's greatness is often measured by the richness of culture that it offers those who live there.

Many people choose to live in cities for economic reasons. Cities offer a variety of jobs and other economic opportunities. Many city dwellers have found prosperity through trade. Nearly all the world's great cities were founded on trade—the voluntary exchange of goods and services between people. The great cities remain major economic centers.

City living can, of course, have its disadvantages. Despite these disadvantages, cities continue to thrive. By reading about the people, culture, geography, and economy of various metropolitan centers, you will understand why. You will also understand why the world is becoming more and more urban. Finally, you will learn what it is that makes each world city unique.

Mark Schug, Consulting Editor
Co-author of *Teaching Social Studies in the Elementary School* and *Community Study*

CONSULTING EDITOR

Mark C. Schug
Professor of Curriculum and Instruction
University of Wisconsin—Milwaukee

EDITORIAL

Amy Bauman, Project Editor
Barbara J. Behm
Judith Smart, Editor-in-Chief

ART/PRODUCTION

Suzanne Beck, Art Director
Carole Kramer, Designer
Thom Pharmakis, Photo Researcher
Eileen Rickey, Typesetter
Andrew Rupniewski, Production Manager

Reviewed for accuracy by:
Richard Kraft
Social Studies Department Chair
Los Altos High School
Hacienda Heights, California

Library of Congress Number: 89-10467

2 3 4 5 6 7 8 9   96 95 94 93 92

Library of Congress Cataloging in Publication Data

Davis, James E., 1940-
  Los Angeles.
  (World cities)
  Summary: Explores the history, cultural heritage, demographics, geography, and economic and natural resources of Los Angeles.
  1. Los Angeles (Calif.)—Juvenile literature. [1. Los Angeles (Calif.)] I. Hawke, Sharryl Davis. II. Title. III. Series: Davis, James E., 1940- . World cities.
F869.L857D38 1989   979.4′94   [B] [92]   89-10467
ISBN 0-8172-3028-9 (lib. bdg.)

Cover Photo: Image Bank/Brett Froomer

LOS ANGELES

WORLD CITIES

JAMES E. DAVIS
AND
SHARRYL DAVIS HAWKE

RAINTREE
STECK-VAUGHN
LIBRARY

Austin, Texas

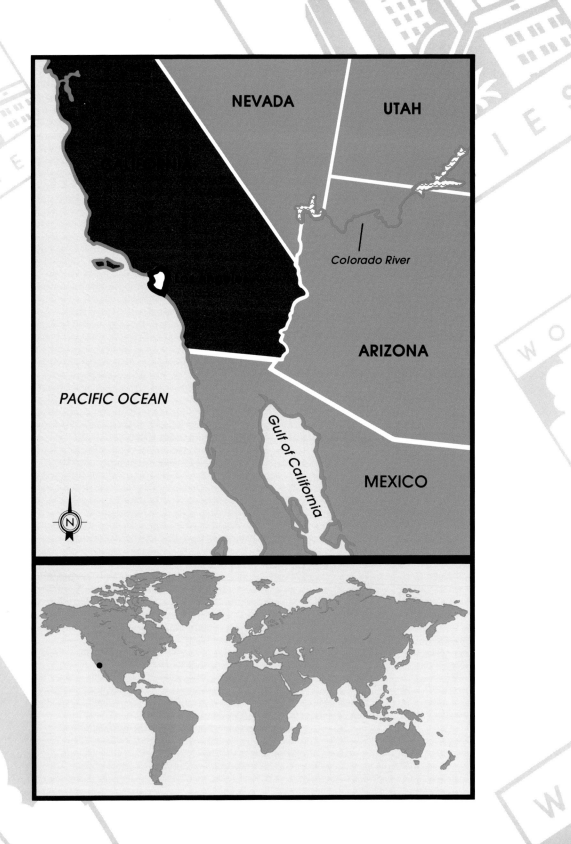

Contents

Introduction

The Setting

Picture Los Angeles in your mind. Chances are you see sunny beaches and surfers. Perhaps you see movie cameras and spotlights or Disneyland rides and rock stars. Or maybe you even picture miles and miles of freeways with cars whizzing by in all directions.

Los Angeles is all of this and more. L.A., as it is sometimes called, is a city of fantasy where dreams are said to come true. You will see many familiar names and places as you read about Los Angeles—Hollywood, Mickey Mouse, Beverly Hills, Universal Studios, Malibu. Los Angeles has become familiar to most people because many movies and television shows are filmed here.

Have you ever watched the television shows "L.A. Law" or "Hunter"? These are only a couple of many television shows and films that have been set in Los Angeles. If you've watched these shows you may have seen the wide, sandy beaches; the skyscrapers; or the expensive homes that are common in the city. You may have caught glimpses of the marinas where the big sailboats are docked or seen cars crisscrossing the freeways. All of these are everyday scenes in Los Angeles.

Films are often made in Los Angeles because the weather is so nice. This is partly because the city is so far south. The summers are warm, and the winters are mild, so you rarely need a winter coat in this city. You would need a bathing suit more often. The

Not all of Los Angeles is palm trees and beaches. Skyscrapers now fill the downtown (opposite).

7

sun shines most of the time, so people do many things outdoors. They can swim, surf, sail, build sand castles, visit the zoo, and play sports practically all year round.

The Pacific Ocean helps make the weather in Los Angeles nice, too. The ocean is so big that it never gains or loses much heat. The constant ocean temperatures keep the air from getting too cold or too hot. The Pacific borders Los Angeles to the west and to the south.

The sun shines so much that flowers grow in Los Angeles all year round. These flowers come in all the colors of the rainbow. They dot the cliffs by the ocean. They bloom on people's lawns. They sprout from flower boxes on city streets. They even grow alongside some of the freeways.

Palm trees also line the roads and freeways. Some are short and stubby and look like giant pineapples. Others are tall and stately. Orange trees grow on people's lawns, too. Some people even have avocado trees. Imagine eating oranges and avocados that you can pick right off your own trees. The cactus plants that grow around Los Angeles are just like those that grow in the nearby desert. In the springtime, the city comes alive when the beautiful cactus flowers bloom.

Los Angeles is located in southern California. It is the center of Los Angeles County, which is one of fifty-eight counties in the state. Los Angeles County includes eighty-five different communities and cities. Some people describe this county as an "urban sprawl." All of the cities have spread out and run into each other. It is hard to tell where one city ends and the next begins. Los Angeles County is also called the Los Angeles Metropolitan Area. An even larger area, called Greater Los Angeles, includes parts of four other counties. Los Angeles County covers 4,083 square miles (10,575 sq. kilometers). This area is bigger than the states of Rhode Island and Delaware combined.

Almost everyone in Los Angeles travels by car. There are more than 650 miles (1,050 km) of freeways in the city and many more surrounding it. This gives Los Angeles one of the world's largest freeway systems. In fact, California has more miles of freeways than any other state.

Because cars are so important in Los Angeles, many automobile trends begin there. For example, the people of Los Angeles were the first to have vanity license plates. These are licenses that use initials, nicknames, or funny words instead of random letters and numbers. Sunroofs and cardboard windshield visors also started here.

There are many ways to have fun if you live in or visit Los Angeles. Along

Many Los Angeles autos have vanity license plates. The owner of this car obviously considers it a work of art.

with the beaches and mountains, Los Angeles has art museums, theaters, amusement parks, and sports arenas. For these reasons, people come from all over the world to visit Los Angeles. Presently, about 46 million people visit the city every year. Many of them come by airplane. They fly into Los Angeles International Airport, called LAX for short. About 400,000 planes travel to and take off from LAX every year.

The People

London, England, is a very old European city. New York City and Boston are considered old American cities. Compared to London, New York, and Boston, Los Angeles is a very new city. Most of the people in Los Angeles have come only in this century. In the past thirty years, for example, Los Angeles has grown by almost three million people. More people now live in Los Angeles than in

9

©Arthur Threadgill

any other city in the United States except for New York. Los Angeles continues its rapid growth. Experts say that it will have more people than New York by the early 1990s. Already, about thirteen million people live in Greater Los Angeles. Eight and a half million of these people live in Los Angeles County. Only eight of the fifty states in the country have more people than Los Angeles County.

The people of Los Angeles come from many different cultures. They may speak Spanish, Chinese, or Japanese. More than half of them are black, Asian, or Hispanic. All of them call Los Angeles home.

About one out of every three people in the city is Hispanic. Some of them are descendants of Spanish settlers. Others have parents or grandparents who came to Los Angeles from Mexico. Some came from other countries of Latin America. Many Hispanics speak English, but others speak only Spanish. Even though most of them are American citizens, they still remember the rich traditions of their culture. Mexican fiestas are held all over the city on Cinco de Mayo, or the "Fifth of May." This holiday celebrates the day in 1862 when Mexican forces defeated the French army.

Los Angeles is made rich by the cultures of its many ethnic groups. In the Hispanic neighborhood shown here, a street vendor sells food.

All of these different cultures combine to make Los Angeles a very lively place. Hispanics, blacks, and Asians have made important contributions to Los Angeles. Some are government leaders. Mayor Thomas Bradley was the first black mayor of Los Angeles. He has been mayor since 1973. Others are famous artists, musicians, writers, or actors. They own many kinds of businesses. In fact, Los Angeles has more black-owned businesses than any other United States city.

The Problems

Los Angeles is not really one city. It is many cities. Any large city with such a mixture of people faces many problems, and Los Angeles is no exception. Angelenos, as the city's people are called, must work hard to solve the problems they face. The freeways and roads are crowded. The air and water are polluted. Because of the warm weather, many homeless people come to Los Angeles. They wander the streets, often begging for money. The city's homeless population has grown in recent years. Because of this, some cities around Los Angeles have shelters for homeless people.

Los Angeles also has a problem with crime. Crime is a problem all over Los Angeles, but the most dangerous areas are in Hollywood and in South-Central Los Angeles. Thousands of violent crimes are committed every year. Street gangs fight each other. Drug abuse is a big problem. There are so many criminals that prisons are over-crowded.

The city's mild climate draws many homeless people to Los Angeles. Here, homeless people wait for a free meal outside a downtown shelter.

©Arthur Threadgill

Geography

Everyone in Los Angeles is planning for "the big one"—that is, the big earthquake. Los Angeles is in an earthquake zone that has been trembling for about 65 million years. Scientists think that a major earthquake will hit California about once every 160 years.

You probably practice fire drills in your school. Los Angeles schoolchildren have fire drills too, but they also have earthquake drills. In these drills, students are taught to "drop." When this word is shouted or when an earthquake is felt, students immediately climb under their desks. The desks would help protect the children if the building should start to crumble during an earthquake.

In middle school and high school, students often learn first aid. In a disaster such as an earthquake, the students could give emergency first aid until ambulances and medical help arrived. Their training might save the lives of their fellow students.

When big earthquakes hit cities, many people can be killed or injured. Walls in buildings crack, and some buildings fall down. Power lines and water lines are often damaged. Telephones may go out of order. Sometimes rockslides cause rocks on the hillsides and cliffs to tumble down. Roads are damaged. When this happens, fire engines and ambulances have trouble getting to places where they are needed.

Officials in Los Angeles and the rest of California have a safety plan to follow if a big earthquake hits. They work with hospitals so that everyone will know what to do if people are injured. Plans have been made for emergency food and water. Ideas for transportation are discussed. A radio system is being set up so that all emergency aid people can still communicate. The county government spent $47 million in 1988 to prepare for earthquakes and other major disasters.

Today, Los Angeles's skyscrapers are built with special techniques to help make them "earthquake-proof." Maybe they could withstand a big earthquake. But no one is sure just how safe they really are.

How Earthquakes Happen

Earthquakes occur because California straddles two big pieces of land that scrape against each other. The crack between the two pieces of land is called the San Andreas Fault. The piece of land on the west side of the fault is called the Pacific Plate. It moves slowly northward. The piece of land east of the fault is called the North American Plate. It moves slowly to the south. The San Andreas Fault lies north of Los Angeles. While this fault is capable of causing "the big one," other very serious fault lines run directly below the city.

One other famous California city is San Francisco. This city is in northern California and lies east of the fault. Los Angeles is west of the fault. These two cities move closer together every time the fault shifts. Scientists estimate that they move about 2 inches (5 centimeters) closer together every year.

Earthquakes of the Past

Not every earthquake causes damage. People in Los Angeles experience many small earthquakes every year. In small earthquakes everything shakes for a moment. Dishes rattle in cupboards. Lamps may fall off tables. The commotion lasts for a few seconds. Then everything settles down, and people go back to what they were doing.

Following a 1971 earthquake, rescuers carry bodies from the rubble of a hospital.

But several big earthquakes have hit Los Angeles in the past. The San Andreas Fault made major movements in 1855 and 1857. These earthquakes nearly destroyed Los Angeles. The earthquake of 1857 was particularly strong. It measured 8.3 on the Richter scale. The Richter scale is a system that scientists use to measure the strength of an earthquake. Earthquakes that measure more than 7.0 on the Richter scale are considered severe. So you can imagine how powerful the earthquakes of 1855 and 1857 were.

A bigger earthquake hit Los Angeles in 1933. One hundred and twenty people were killed, and the earthquake caused $41 million in damage. In 1971, an earthquake shook an area of Los Angeles called the San Fernando Valley. It measured 6.6 on the Richter scale, and sixty-four people were killed. This earthquake caused over $1 billion in damage.

In 1987, an earthquake hit the Whittier Narrows area of Los Angeles. It measured 5.9 on the Richter scale. Six people died, and two hundred minor injuries were reported.

Earthquakes Shape California

Earthquakes have helped to shape the land around Los Angeles. Millions of years ago, the land on which Los

Angeles is built was underwater. It was still part of the ocean. But volcanoes erupted under the water, spreading melted rock, or lava. The lava began to pile up on the ocean floor. The layers and layers of lava and soil stacked up, slowly adding to the land. As sea animals died, they too helped to build up the land. The Los Angeles area is now rich with oil deposits because of all the sea animals that were

mixed with the layers of soil millions of years ago.

As the land built up, the plates started to move under the weight. They pushed against each other causing pressure along their edges. This pressure led to earthquakes that buckled the land. In this way, mountains formed. Eventually, the land rose above sea level. The mountains that formed in this way are called the Los Angeles

The same forces that cause California's earthquakes have also created Los Angeles's unique mountain setting.

Ranges. These ranges are also sometimes called the Transverse Ranges because they run from east to west. The other mountain ranges in California run from north to south. The Los Angeles Ranges include the San Gabriel, the Santa Monica, the Santa Ynez, and the San Bernardino mountains.

A model at the La Brea Tar Pits shows how prehistoric animals were trapped in the sticky pools.

Changes During the Ice Age

The earth has experienced several great ice ages since time began. An ice age occurs when the average temperatures around the earth drop by just a few degrees. The last great ice age started about one and a half million years ago and lasted until about nine thousand years ago. This ice age is called the Pleistocene Ice Age. *Pleistocene* means "most recent."

During this ice age, great sheets of ice formed over the northern parts of the northern continents. The sheets of ice, called glaciers, advanced and retreated four times. The glaciers never reached the area that is now Los Angeles. The Los Angeles area was cool and wet. Many rivers, streams, and lakes formed. The vegetation was lush and plentiful. Animals from the northern part of the continent migrated to this area.

Los Angeles has a special place called the La Brea Tar Pits that is a rich source of prehistoric fossils. Fossils can be animal bones or hardened plant parts. They can also be imprints of plants or animals preserved in a hardened surface. The La Brea Tar Pits were formed by pools of oil that bubbled to the earth's surface through fault lines. This oil, which was very sticky like glue or taffy, was covered by a pool of water. Prehistoric animals coming to drink from the water were often trapped in the sticky oil. When they could not get out, they died there. The oil and tar preserved the dead animals' bones.

The early settlers used tar from the pits on the roofs of their houses. They saw the bones but thought they were just from common animals. Little did they know that the bones belonged to animals that lived more than nine thousand years ago. Since the beginning of this century, however, scientists have spent much time studying these fossils. In some cases they have even pieced the bones together like a puzzle. They have put together skeletons of mammoths, saber-toothed tigers, and many other prehistoric animals.

Even the bones of an ancient woman have been found in the pits. Scientists think the woman was about thirty years old and lived about nine thousand years ago. They named her the La Brea Woman. You can see many fossils, including the bones of the La Brea Woman, if you visit the Page Museum next to the tar pits today.

The Desert

After the Ice Age, the air warmed. Rivers and streams dried up. Many different kinds of animals died out because their environment changed. The Los Angeles area is still in this stage today. The air is very dry, and there is not much water in the area. In fact, Los Angeles has a very desert-like climate today. Water is brought to Los Angeles from faraway places through aqueducts. Aqueducts are pipes, channels, or other systems used to move water from one place to another. Some of the water is brought from the eastern slopes of the Sierra Mountains in northern California. Some is brought from the Colorado River on the border of California and

Arizona. Still, there are water shortages sometimes, especially in the dry

In a display at the Page Museum, an image of what the La Brea Woman may have looked like is projected behind her skeleton.

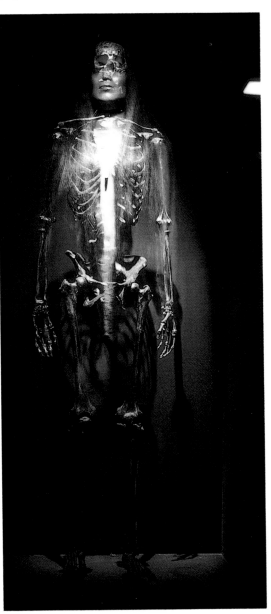

©Arthur Threadgill

summer months. Everyone is encouraged to use as little water as possible.

Wind and Rain

Two other elements of nature that make Los Angeles a unique place to live are the winds and the heavy rains. The winds are called the Santa Anas. They come from the desert and move across the mountains and through the canyons and valleys to the coastline. Along the way, they usually clear the Los Angeles area of smog, driving it out to sea. Coming from the desert, however, the winds also add to the city's heat, especially in the summer months. They dry the landscape. Because it rarely rains in the summertime, the trees, shrubs, and grasses get very dry. Burning cigarettes or even small sparks may cause a fire. The Santa Anas then fan the fires and spread them around. These great brush fires have destroyed many homes and have even caused death.

Although it rarely rains in the summertime, it sometimes rains for days and days in the winter. California's rainy season begins in November and lasts until about April. If the rain lasts too long, mudslides can occur. Mudslides can cause much damage and even push houses into the sea. It doesn't always rain in the winter, though. Some winters are very dry.

Exhaust from millions of cars on Los Angeles roads and freeways causes nearly three-fourths of the city's air pollution.

Living with the Smog

One bad thing about Los Angeles that nobody likes is the smog. The word smog is a combination of "smoke" and "fog." Smog is created by people. It is the dirty air made from chemicals released into the environment. It comes from the exhaust fumes from the millions of cars on the Los Angeles freeways. It also comes from factories that release pollution into the air.

The location of the mountains and the weather patterns around Los Angeles cause smog to hang over the city and surrounding area. The mountains keep the smog from blowing away. It lingers over Los Angeles, trapped over the city. Heavy smog makes it hard to see very far. Everything seems covered in a yellowish brown haze. Even people who live close to the mountains may not see them for days. When the smog is this thick, people's eyes may burn, or they may have trouble breathing. Worse yet, smog damages plants and crops.

On heavy smog days, officials warn people not to spend too much time outdoors. Radio stations broadcast "smog alert" warnings for elderly people and joggers to be especially careful. During smog alerts, students are not allowed to participate in organized sports or have active recesses at school. City officials are trying hard to control and reduce the smog. Cars are now made with parts that limit the exhaust fumes. People are encouraged to reduce driving on heavy smog days. It is not likely that this problem will be solved very soon, but the people are learning. They know that with the beautiful mountains, valleys, beaches, and desert, there is much to protect in Los Angeles.

The mountains surrounding Los Angeles often trap polluted air over the city. The heavy haze that results is called smog.

©Arthur Threadgill

Life in the Past

When you look at Los Angeles today you see tall skyscrapers, expensive homes, and miles of freeways. But long ago Los Angeles looked very different. Before the Spaniards came, it was an Indian village. Indians walked along trails that are now freeways. Their grass huts stood where expensive homes now stand. The ocean where they paddled their canoes is now traveled by huge ships.

Several different Indian tribes made their home in the area beginning about 1,500 years ago. One tribe, the Shoshones, lived in a village called Yang-na. Yang-na was near where downtown Los Angeles is today. Other Indian tribes lived in small villages on the beaches and in the valleys. The

Indians ate acorns, berries, seeds, and fish.

When Los Angeles Was El Pueblo

All of this changed after the Spanish explorers arrived. The Spaniards first made an expedition into southern California in 1769. Captain Gaspar de Portolá and a priest named Juan Crespi led the expedition. Crespi wrote in his diary that he thought the area that is now Los Angeles was the perfect site for a settlement. The expedition moved on toward Yang-na. There the explorers met a group of Indians. The Indian chief brought the men beads made of shells. His tribe used the beads in the same way as money is

Father Juan Crespi helped lead the first Spanish expedition into southern California. According to Crespi's diary, California's first baptism was performed in 1769.

used today. Crespi gave the Indians tobacco and glass beads in exchange for some of the shell beads.

The king of Spain soon ordered the colonization of California. Spanish priests began to establish missions along the coast. Father Junípero Serra led the way, building the first near modern-day San Diego. The priests wanted to convert the Indians to Christianity. The priests would teach the Indians how to raise cattle and sheep and how to grow wheat, corn, and beans. They would also give them religious lessons.

The missions always included a large church surrounded by areas for daily living as well as gardens, orchards, and pastures where animals could graze.

Eventually, twenty-one missions were established along the California coast. Mission San Gabriel and Mission San Fernando Rey de España were established near what is now Los Angeles.

As the next step in the colonization process, the Spanish governor of California, Felipe de Neve, decided to establish towns. The first town was built at the Yang-na site in 1781. De Neve's solidiers recruited eleven families from Mexico who wanted to live in the new town. They were promised free land, horses, and farm animals if they promised to stay for at least ten years. The eleven families who agreed to settle the new colony included Spaniards, Indians, blacks, mulattos (mixed white and black ancestry), and mestizos (mixed Spanish and Indian ancestry). The settlers' journey from Mexico to California took seven months.

The settlers named the new town *El Pueblo de Nuestra Señora la Reina de Los Angeles,* which means "The Town of Our Lady the Queen of the Angels." It was called El Pueblo for short. First they built huts made of grass and mud. But soon they built adobe homes.

Life in the pueblo was hard. Everyone had to pitch in to help with the work, even the older boys and girls. Some people took care of the cattle and sheep. Others worked in the fields and harvested the crops. There was little time for school or play.

All the hard work paid off handsomely. The town was very successful and grew quickly. After five years, the families received official title to the land they had been promised. It was not long before the settlers became wealthy *rancheros,* or ranchers. By the 1820s, El Pueblo had a general store and a church. By 1836, over 2,200 people lived in the town. The United States Government Federal Building now stands at the site of the first general store at Temple and Main streets.

From Mexican Territory to American State

Mexico won its independence from Spain in 1821. In the following year,

Los Angeles and all of California came under Mexican rule, too. This meant that the Spanish governor of California would be replaced by a Mexican governor. Many people in the pueblo of Los Angeles rebelled against this. For one thing, they wanted Los Angeles to be the capital instead of Monterey. This city had been the capital even under Spanish rule. They also did not want outsiders governing them.

The rebels caused a great deal of trouble for the string of governors sent by Mexico. A group led by Pío Pico gained control in 1845. This rebel leader became the new governor. Pico, however, was to be the last Mexican governor of California. American soldiers marched into Los Angeles in 1846 and took control of the city.

Tension had been growing between the United States and Mexico. In May of 1846, the United States declared war on Mexico. Commodore Robert F. Stockton and his soldiers arrived on a ship and raised the American flag on San Pedro's beach. San Pedro is where the Port of Los Angeles is now.

The American invasion took Los Angeles by surprise. Although both the Americans and the Mexicans living in the area were restless under the Mexican rule, they did not necessarily want to become part of the United States. Still, the rancheros were not ready to fight when Stockton and his soldiers marched into Los Angeles in August 1846. But by mid-September, the leaders of Los Angeles had gathered soldiers and ammunition. They staged a surprise attack against the Americans. The Americans fled to the beach and escaped on a ship.

When the Americans returned with more soldiers, the Californians again chased them away. Finally, Commodore Stockton came back to Los Angeles with six hundred soldiers. After another long battle, the Californians surrendered in January 1847. A year later, the Mexican War ended with Mexico's defeat. By the Treaty of Guadalupe Hidalgo, Mexico gave California and a huge section of what is now the American southwest to the United States. California became a state in 1850.

The Plight of the Indians

Even before this, most of the Indians from Yang-na and the other villages had joined the missions. Mission life seemed attractive to them at the time because they could learn how to raise livestock and crops. But over the years, many of the Indians forgot their customs and traditions. The Indian children were not learning the skills their parents had known before the settlers came.

In 1833, the Mexican governor of California had abolished the missions and sent away priests. This left the Indians to fend for themselves. But after living in the missions, the Indian people were poor and had nowhere to go. Worse yet, they could not return to their old customs because their culture had been ruined. Besides, they had no land.

Commodore Robert Stockton led the United States forces that landed near Los Angeles during the Mexican War.

L.A. County Natural History Museum

Some Indians took jobs with the rancheros. The rancheros did not treat the Indians fairly. They paid them only a few dollars for a whole year of work. Because of this, the Indians became like slaves to the wealthy rancheros. Other Indians found jobs in the town. These people also received very little money for their work. Many Indians could not find jobs at all.

The Indians faced another problem too—illness. They had not been exposed to many diseases before the settlers came. They caught the settlers' diseases very easily and often died. More than six thousand Indians who died of smallpox and cholera epidemics in 1825 are buried at the Mission San Gabriel.

The missions fell into ruin after they were abandoned. The Mexicans sold the mission lands to the rancheros piece by piece until there was nothing

A museum display shows Mission San Gabriel during Mexican rule.

left. The buildings were neglected and started to fall apart. Today, however, the missions have been restored so that visitors can see what mission life was like.

From Pueblo to Modern City

Los Angeles grew quickly after California became a state. The first spurt of growth came with the California gold rush in 1849. In 1842, Don Francisco Lopez discovered gold while digging up wild onions near his home in the San Fernando Valley. But even more gold was discovered in northern California near San Francisco in 1848. This discovery brought the "forty-niners" (named for the year 1849) to the new state. About 100,000 men rushed into San Francisco seeking gold and riches.

Many men from Los Angeles went north as well. But they soon realized that the riches they were seeking could be found at home—not from gold, but from beef. The forty-niners needed to eat. Rancheros from Los Angeles provided beef. The price of cattle and other food skyrocketed. The Los Angeles rancheros became even wealthier. Some of them built large brick houses and rode in horse-drawn carriages instead of wooden carts. A man named Don Abel Stearns caused townspeople to gossip by bringing the first carriage to Los Angeles. They said he was trying to impress his young wife.

But in 1861, this period of growth came to an end. It rained for days and days. After more than 50 inches (127 centimeters) of rain fell, Los Angeles was waist-deep in floods. Many cattle died. As if this wasn't enough, a drought struck the area from 1862 to 1864, and more cattle died. The rancheros had to sell their land in order to pay off their debts.

It was a bad time for the rancheros, but a good time for everyone else. Now other people could buy plots of land. Many of the forty-niners came to Los Angeles from the north. Americans from other parts of the country streamed in. These people started farms. They grew oranges and other fruits and vegetables. Most of the valleys around Los Angeles were filled with orange groves at this time.

A new period of growth started. Pío Pico, the former governor, built the city's first hotel. This huge hotel, called the Pico House, was begun in 1869. In 1874, streetcars were introduced. These streetcars were actually horse-drawn carts. People were charged a small fee to ride in them. The first electric trolley began running about thirteen years later.

For long distance travel, a railroad connected San Francisco and Los Angeles by 1876. Two other railroads

The Plaza and Pico Heights Electric Line was Los Angeles's first electric trolley.

linked the city to the rest of the country by 1887. The railroads brought even more people to Los Angeles. This period was called the Great Boom. The population rose to 50,000 by 1890 and to 100,000 by 1900. The railroad also made it easier for farmers in Los Angeles to sell their crops in other cities.

For some time, oil prospecting boomed in California. Prospectors combed the Los Angeles area for this "black gold" without much luck. This changed when inexperienced prospectors Edward L. Doheny and Charles Canfield began to drill in in the city's residential area. There, in 1892, they discovered huge pools of oil. This set off an excitement like that of the gold rush. Many people discovered oil on their own property; some even became rich. Oil production became an important industry.

Los Angeles had electric streetlights by 1882. It was not long before electricity and telephones were common. Construction began on the Port of Los Angeles in 1899. Los Angeles would soon become an important port city trading with nations around the world. The city was on its way to becoming one of the biggest in the United States.

The Twentieth Century

Los Angeles continued to grow rapidly at the turn of the century. In 1902, engineers built an aqueduct to supply the growing city with water. The Los Angeles Aqueduct was built in Owens Valley, north of the city. It carried water from the snow-covered mountains near the valley across 250 miles (402 km) of desert to the city.

The electric trolley system expanded. Angelenos could ride the big cars to the beach or to work. For the first time, people could live in one place and work in another. Commuting to work became a way of life. The electric trolley cars rode on rails and were powered by overhead electric lines. The power was transferred to the car by means of a long pole.

It was at this time that a new industry brought fame and fortune to the city—the movie business. William Selig started the movie industry in Los Angeles. He was making a movie in Chicago in 1907 when bad weather forced him to stop filming. He sent a crew to Los Angeles to finish the movie. The mild weather allowed the crew to film whenever they wanted to. Nearby mountains, deserts, and beaches gave them different settings to film. Other movie makers soon followed. Movie stars began making their homes in Hollywood and Beverly Hills.

This gigantic structure was built for the 1917 movie Intolerance. *A camera dangling from a hot-air balloon was used to film scenes on this set.*

About this time, the country experienced the Great Depression. The Great Depression of the 1930s was a period of time in which business slowed down all over America. Entire companies closed down. People lost their jobs. Churches had to set up "soup kitchens" to feed hungry families. Thousands of people streamed into California looking for jobs. But there were few jobs to be found.

By the 1930s, the motion picture business had become very important. Hollywood was the place where most movies were made. The strength of this industry carried Los Angeles through the Great Depression. It provided jobs even when jobs were hard to find in other places. It also brought tourists to the city. Everyone wanted to meet the stars. They wanted to walk the streets where their favorite actors and actresses had walked. They wanted to see the stars' homes. The motion picture business is still providing jobs today. Tourists still swarm to Hollywood to be near their favorite stars.

On December 7, 1941, many Angelenos were enjoying a Sunday drive or relaxing at home. They were shocked to hear on their radios that Japan had bombed Pearl Harbor in Hawaii. That was the day that the United States really entered World War II. Los Angeles, like other cities, would be greatly changed by the war.

During the depression, the motion-picture industry continued to grow. Here, movie star Ginger Rogers signs an impression of her dancing feet outside Mann's Chinese Theater in 1939.

Los Angeles became a center for the defense industry. Because of this change, the city's economy boomed again. Factories made aircraft, tanks, and other weapons needed for the war. When many of the city's men were drafted into the military, women took their places in the factories.

At that time there were forty thousand people of Japanese ancestry living in Los Angeles. These people were Americans, but many people blamed them for the war. Some of these Japanese-Americans were mistreated by former neighbors and friends. Many were taken prisoner by the United States government. It was a sad time for the Japanese-Americans.

The following months were filled with frightening air raid drills. Alarms would sound and people would have to see that all lights were out. Because of Los Angeles's location on the Pacific Ocean, many people thought it would be attacked just like Pearl Harbor was.

They thought that if they turned out all the lights in the city, pilots in the enemy planes and submarines would not be able to see their targets.

Los Angeles was never attacked. The closest call came in February 1942. A Japanese submarine surfaced near Santa Barbara and shot at an oil plant on the coast. Santa Barbara is a city about 90 miles (145 km) north of Los Angeles. No one was hurt, and California was never attacked again.

The end of the war in 1945 brought new problems. Many people had moved to the city to fill jobs in the

During World War II, 112,000 Japanese-Americans living on the West Coast were forced into prison camps like this one in Owens Valley. The United States government has since agreed to pay the former prisoners for their suffering and loss of property.

defense industry. With the war over, there would be no jobs. Soldiers were returning home. They needed work and places to live. Some 162,000 families, including 50,000 soldiers, were living in tents, garages, cabins, trailers, and old hotels. The government had to step in with money for housing and job programs to help these people. Soon Los Angeles began to prosper again.

After the war, the defense industry continued to grow. The city became a center for other industries as well. The new industries brought even more people to Los Angeles. By 1960, the

Over 650 miles (1,050 km) of freeways help tie together the sprawl of Los Angeles and its suburbs.

population of Los Angeles County had risen to 6 million people. By 1970, there were 7 million people, and by 1980, almost 7.5 million people were counted. By 1989, an estimated 8.5 million people lived in this county.

With the influx of even more people and businesses, the suburbs of Los Angeles have sprawled out wider and wider. Skyscrapers have emerged. More and more freeways have been built to handle all the traffic.

Los Angeles will continue to grow and change. It started out as a tiny settlement of eleven families. Those men and women could never have imagined what Los Angeles would be like today. It makes you wonder. What will Los Angeles be like in another 250 years?

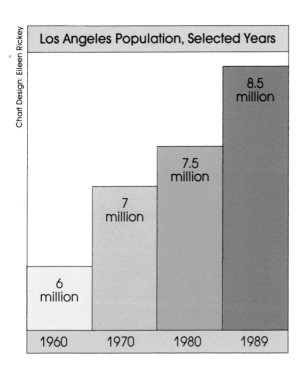

Since 1960, Los Angeles's population has grown by more than 2.5 million people.

WORLD CITIES

Regions of the City

Los Angeles is a city of contrasts. It is made up of many regions, each of which has a distinct flavor. Los Angeles is sometimes described as a city without a center. Other American cities are like the cities of Europe. They are called "walking cities." A walking city has a downtown area surrounded by suburbs. The suburbs are mainly for homes, while the businesses and government buildings are concentrated in the downtown area.

Los Angeles is different. Greater Los Angeles is made up of many cities. Each has its own center. All of them have businesses, offices, and government buildings. They are equal in many ways to downtown Los Angeles. Many of them have skyscrapers and crowded streets. This is why the Los Angeles area is referred to as an urban sprawl.

The biggest spurt of growth for Los Angeles came after the invention of the automobile. Angelenos fell in love with the automobile. People didn't mind driving a long way to commute to work. The freedom to move around caused many mini-cities to spring up. Still, downtown Los Angeles has remained an important part of Greater Los Angeles.

Downtown Los Angeles

The heart of downtown Los Angeles started out as the settlers' first homestead. It now boasts stately government buildings as well as elegant theaters, museums, and art galleries. It is home to the people of many different cultures.

City and county government buildings are located in the core of downtown. Los Angeles City Hall at Temple and Spring streets is where the city goverment offices are located. The city's tallest skyscraper, the United California Building, is near here. It is sixty-two stories tall.

The Westin Bonaventure Hotel is another interesting building. This modern building looks like it could be from a science fiction movie about the future. There are 5 acres (2 ha) of waterfalls and ponds *inside* this hotel.

The Music Center, with three famous theaters, is close by. One of these three theaters is the Dorothy Chandler Pavilion. The Academy Awards are held at this theater every year. It is also where the Los Angeles Philharmonic Orchestra often plays. Los Angeles Theatre Center, with four smaller theaters, is just a few blocks south.

If you walk the streets of downtown Los Angeles, you will hear many languages. You will smell the aroma of tasty foreign foods. This is especially true in three special neighborhoods of Los Angeles—Olvera Street, Little Tokyo, and Chinatown.

The Hispanic community is built around Olvera Street. This street is the oldest one in the city. The oldest stand-ing house in Los Angeles is located at 14 Olvera Street. The first Catholic church in Los Angeles is also here. The Old Plaza Church, as it is known, has held religious services since 1822. The Old Plaza Fire House was the city's first firehouse. It now houses a museum with antique firefighting equipment.

The thirty-five-story Westin Bonaventure Hotel houses an indoor pond in a lobby the size of a city block.

©Arthur Threadgill

Olvera Street, the site of a Mexican-style market, contains the city's oldest buildings.

You can stroll through a Mexican-style market on Olvera Street. Vendors sell Mexican piñatas and other crafts, including handwoven blankets and brightly colored clothing. Restaurants serve homemade tortillas and tacos. Mexican dancers and musicians entertain the public.

Little Tokyo is a Japanese neighborhood just south of Olvera Street. This community is one hundred years old. The buildings here have turned-up rooftops just like buildings in Japan. The building signs are written in

Diners enjoy Japanese food in Little Tokyo (above). The handprints and footprints of well-known entertainers cover the sidewalk outside Mann's Chinese Theater (below).

Japanese, and people on the streets often speak in Japanese. A mass of shops and restaurants offer visitors a bit of Japanese culture.

Chinatown is near Little Tokyo. This colorful area is full of shops that sell Chinese clothing, food, and other items. Restaurants serve all sorts of delicious Chinese food. Because of the heavy Chinese influence, many signs on the buildings are written in Chinese characters. As you walk among Chinatown's people, you will hear many people speaking in Chinese.

Farmer's Market and Grand Central Market are other good places for hungry people to go. Both of these large, open-air markets sell fresh fruits and vegetables as well as exotic treats and gourmet foods. Here, too, is the Los Angeles Flower Market. This flower market is the largest in the United States.

The Lights of Hollywood

Heading west out of downtown Los Angeles, you will pass through Hollywood. Before the 1900s, Hollywood was farmland for citrus fruits, watermelon, bell peppers, and other crops. In 1911, Hollywood became the site of the first motion-picture studio. This studio, built by the Nestor Film Company, set Hollywood at the center of the entire motion-picture industry.

One of the most famous streets in Hollywood is Hollywood Boulevard. Mann's Chinese Theater (formerly

Mann's Chinese Theater (above) was the scene of many movie premieres in the 1920s and 1930s. Gold stars engraved with famous names line Hollywood's fifteen-block Walk of Fame (right).

Grauman's Chinese Theater) is on this street. The sidewalk running just outside this theater is embedded with the handprints and footprints of many of Hollywood's movie stars. Another famous stretch of sidewalk is the Walk of Fame at the intersection of Hollywood and Vine. This sidewalk celebrates Hollywood's entertainers with bronze stars. About 1,800 bronze stars are now part of the walk.

Another famous street is Sunset Boulevard. Along this strip hundreds of fancy billboards advertise the newest movies and record albums. The section of Wilshire Boulevard between Vermont and La Brea avenues is called the "Miracle Mile." Law firms, advertising agencies, and other important businesses are located here.

The "Hollywood" sign on the slopes of Hollywood Hills is a famous landmark in Los Angeles. This sign, built in 1922, spells out the city's name in huge letters. It was originally used to advertise homes for sale in the area. Laurel Canyon was one of Hollywood's first residential canyons. Many rock

The "Hollywood" sign has come to symbolize the world's motion-picture capital. The sign, which was built in the 1920s to promote a real-estate company, originally read "Hollywoodland."

singers and movie stars have made their homes in this canyon. Other celebrities live in the Chateau Marmont Hotel at the foot of the canyon. Some of the canyon roads offer a beautiful view of the city. If it is nighttime, the lights of the city shine below like a million stars.

Keep your eyes open in this part of Los Angeles. It's not that unusual to catch a glimpse of a famous movie star. If you see a big limousine with darkened windows, someone famous may be inside. But movie stars and other well-known people can also be seen at sports and cultural events, or even driving along the freeway.

Beverly Hills

Celebrities of all sorts live in Beverly Hills—movie stars, television stars, sports heroes, and other people in the news. You'll know as soon as you pass over the line from Hollywood into Beverly Hills. Busy sidewalks and crowded streets suddenly give way to green parks and huge mansions.

The average home in Beverly Hills is a mansion with a swimming pool and tennis courts. But don't expect to see too much. Most of the homes are protected by high fences, thick trees, and angry guard dogs.

Beverly Hills is also famous for its shopping district on Rodeo Drive. Many well-known shops line Rodeo

Beverly Hills is home to some of Los Angeles's most famous and wealthy residents.

Drive, selling furs, expensive jewelry, and designer clothing.

Century City

Century City is located west of Beverly Hills. Instead of big homes, tall skyscrapers line the roads. Despite the many office buildings Century City has much to offer. It is home to Twentieth Century-Fox Studios, ABC Entertainment Center, and the Shubert Theatre. People go to Century City for dining, theater, movies, and celebrity parties. The community covers 180 acres (73 ha) of land.

Beach Communities

The coast of Los Angeles has 31 miles (50 km) of sandy beaches. Some

©Arthur Threadgill

of the beaches are lined by rugged cliffs. The beaches are filled with people dressed in the latest fashions. They go surfing, sailing, and swimming. They play volleyball on the beach, sunbathe, and whiz around on skateboards showing off newest tricks. Sometimes at night, people gather around bonfires and have cookouts.

Malibu is the most famous of the beach communities. It is also a wealthy community, and many television and movie stars own beach houses here. This stretch of beach is also known for

The big waves at beaches around Los Angeles make the area a surfers' paradise (above). Santa Monica has preserved an elegant amusement park from the 1920s (below).

Carlye Calvin

its natural beauty. Its splendid beaches attract many people. Surf Rider's Beach is a particular favorite among surfers and surfer watchers.

The next stop is Santa Monica. The Santa Monica Pier that stretches out into the ocean features an old-fashioned amusement park. Several movies have been filmed here, including parts of *The Sting*. Santa Monica also provided the setting of the beach blanket movies of the 1950s.

Venice Beach is one of the most colorful of the Los Angeles beaches. Here, outdoor vendors sell clothing, art, and many other items along Ocean Front Walk. Musicians often perform along this walk, and people sometimes stop to watch or even dance to the music. The walkway is also a popular spot for many different sports. People on skateboards and roller skates do difficult tricks on obstacle courses along this walkway. Joggers run along the path. Some people lift weights, play tennis, or join in a game of pick-up basketball in a special recreation area. Other people just stroll along watching all the action.

Marina del Rey is located south of Venice Beach. The marina is the largest artificial harbor in the world. Homes, condominiums, hotels, and restaurants dot the area around the marina, but boats dominate the scene. Big sailboats, cabin cruisers, and boats of all types are docked here. For a small fee, some boats will take tourists on short ocean rides. If you take one of these rides, you might see groups of seals gathered on the rocks. If it is wintertime, watch for whales coming up for a breath of air. This area is on the route for migrating whales. They can be spotted along the coast from January through March.

The Venice Beach boardwalk is a round-the-clock gathering place for skateboarders.

As you travel south, you'll go through some of Los Angeles's older beach communities: Playa del Rey, Manhattan Beach, Redondo Beach, and Hermosa Beach. Manhattan Beach, in particular, is popular for surfing.

Farther south, Long Beach is home to two unusual sights. One is the ocean liner the *Queen Mary*. This giant ship is docked here as a reminder of a time when ships were still the dominant means of trans-continental travel. The *Queen Mary* is one of the most elegant passenger ships ever built. It crossed the Atlantic Ocean more than one thousand times before American businesspeople bought it and docked it.

The Queen Mary *made more than one thousand Atlantic crossings in its time. In 1967, the ship was permanently docked at Long Beach. Its 382 staterooms now serve as a floating hotel.*

The Spruce Goose, *found next door to the* Queen Mary, *is the largest airplane ever built. This wooden craft made a single, mile-long flight in 1947.*

Visitors can now tour the ship and even stay overnight in one of the ship's staterooms.

Another giant of its time is the *Spruce Goose,* which is next door to the *Queen Mary*. This 400,000-ton airplane has the longest wingspan of any airplane ever built. Designed by millionaire Howard Hughes, the *Spruce Goose* made only one flight. In 1947, Hughes flew the plane one mile at a height of 70 feet (21 m) to prove that it could fly.

The San Fernando Valley

Many entertainment businesses are located in the San Fernando Valley. The valley lies inland from the coast and north of Hollywood, Beverly Hills, and downtown Los Angeles. The Burbank Studios, Warner Bros., Columbia, NBC Studios, and Universal Studios are all located in the valley. The term "valley girl" comes from this part of Los Angeles. Well over 250,000 middle-class families live in the valley communities.

Much of Los Angeles's Mexican-American population lives in an area east of the city's downtown. Unemployment and poverty are problems for many of these Angelenos.

East Los Angeles

The area east of downtown Los Angeles is made up of many small barrios. *Barrio* means "neighborhood" in Spanish. As many as nine out of ten people living in some of the barrios are Chicanos. Chicanos are Americans of Mexican descent.

Opportunities for people in the barrios have been very limited. Many of the people do not speak English, and they are often unemployed. Many houses are old and in poor condition. The Chicano leaders of East Los Angeles are working hard to improve conditions for these people.

South-Central Los Angeles

Some areas south of downtown are also in very poor condition. One of these areas is South-Central Los Angeles. Nine out of ten people living in South-Central Los Angeles are black. They have not had the educational opportunities and other advantages that people in other areas have had. One community in this area is named Watts. Watts became famous during the civil rights riots of the 1960s. During six days of rioting in 1965, thirty-four people died and over one thousand were injured.

Places in the City

Visitors to Los Angeles can choose from a wide variety of attractions and activities. They can relax on the beach or roller skate along Ocean Front Walk. They can stroll through Olvera Street, Chinatown, or Little Tokyo. They can look at stars' homes in Beverly Hills or tour one of the television studios. Of course, many visitors to the area choose to spend a day at Disneyland. Many people enjoy visiting the old missions, attending football or baseball games, or visiting museums and theaters.

Spanish Missions

Two of the original Spanish missions are still standing in Los Angeles. One of them, Mission San Gabriel, was badly damaged in the 1987 earthquake. Walls cracked and parts of the ceiling fell down. Some people are now working to restore the mission. It will be closed to the public for a few years.

But you can still tour the Mission San Fernando Rey de España. This mission was damaged by an earthquake in 1818 but was soon repaired. It was founded in 1797. Visitors can imagine what mission life was like for the priests and the 56 Indians who joined the mission. Indian crafts and antique furniture are on display. Visitors can see how the Indians made soap and candles. Beautiful gardens and a fountain make it a pleasant place to spend a morning or an afternoon.

©Arthur Threadgill

Mission San Gabriel, shown above, was the fourth of twenty-one missions founded by Father Junípero Serra. Cracks caused by earthquakes can be seen in the mission's bell tower (opposite page).

The Natural History Museum shows how animals live in their natural environment. It also displays ancient Indian crafts and artifacts. This museum is one of the country's largest natural history museums. It is located in Exposition Park where it is surrounded by picnic grounds and a lovely rose

The Los Angeles County Museum of Art displays thousands of art objects.

Museums

Just about any type of museum can be found in Los Angeles. There are art museums, history museums, science museums, and wax museums.

The biggest art museums are the Museum of Contemporary Art and the Los Angeles County Museum of Art. At the Museum of Contemporary Art, visitors can see famous modern paintings. The Los Angeles County Museum of Art displays art from all over the world. The art, which comes from many different historical periods, includes works of some of the best-known artists. A beautiful garden, filled with interesting sculptures, surrounds the museum. Other nearby museums include the Getty Museum in Malibu, the Norton Simon Museum in Pasadena, and the Page Museum.

garden. Another museum in Exposition Park is the California Museum of Science and Industry. This museum's displays cover a wide variety of scientific topics. Airplanes and satellites are exhibited here. Visitors can learn about robots, see baby chicks hatch, or go for a ride on the General Motors test track.

Several museums in Los Angeles are just for children. The Los Angeles Children's Museum has a make-believe ambulance, a doctor's office, and an emergency room. It also has many toys and books that kids can touch and explore to learn about science, art, and other subjects. Another museum is called Kidspace. Here, kids try on uniforms that people wear in different occupations. They can perform in a television commercial or news show and then see themselves on television. The museum even has a giant tunnel modeled after an ant colony, through which children can climb.

The Hollywood Wax Museum shows wax sculptures of famous movie and television stars. Other museums in the city display crafts and folk art, ancient Greek and Roman sculptures, ancient coins, prehistoric fossils, and valuable manuscripts and books.

Visitors can view wax figures of their favorite entertainers at the Hollywood Wax Museum.

Anaheim Stadium is the home field of the Los Angeles Rams football team (above). The Rams line up for a play (below).

Sports

Los Angeles is a great place for sports. The area's pleasant weather brings people outside to jog, surf, golf, bicycle, and play tennis. But the people of Los Angeles also like to watch sports. Baseball is played at Dodger Stadium and Anaheim Stadium. The Los Angeles Raiders play football at Los Angeles Memorial Coliseum and the Los Angeles Rams play at Anaheim Stadium. Jockeys race thoroughbred horses at Santa Anita Park and at Hollywood Park. The giant Hollywood Park is not just a race track. It covers 350 acres (142 ha) and has a playground, picnic area, and restaurants. The parking lot holds 31,000 cars, and there is room for 32,000 people in the stands.

47

In 1984, Los Angeles was the site of the Summer Olympic Games. Athletes from around the world came to compete for gold, silver, and bronze medals. You can still visit the Olympic Auditorium, where professional boxing matches are now held. You can even stand on the track where athletes set world track records.

A favorite spectator sport for football fans is the Rose Bowl, held every year in January. This big game is held in Pasadena near Los Angeles. Many people camp out the night before to get a good seat for the Tournament of Roses Parade. You've probably seen this parade on television.

Fun and Games

Amusement parks are one of the main attractions in the Los Angeles area. The most famous is Disneyland. Walt Disney, the American film producer, opened Disneyland in 1955. He called it the "happiest place on earth." Many people would agree.

The Tournament of Roses Parade features colorful floats decorated with thousands of flowers.

You could spend all day in Disneyland and still not see everything featured in its seven magical lands. It all starts on Main Street. This street is lined with shops. Tomorrowland looks like a city of the future. Space Mountain takes you on a speeding ride through space. "Captain EO," starring Michael Jackson, is the ultimate in music videos. It uses special effects to create a three-dimensional (3-D) image. The 3-D image seems to come to life if you wear special glasses to watch it.

Storybook characters greet visitors in Fantasyland. You can meet Snow White and the Seven Dwarfs, Mickey Mouse, or Peter Pan. You can tour Sleeping Beauty's castle. In another area of Disneyland, guides take visitors on jungle cruises. You have to watch out for the alligators and hippopotamuses. Frontierland takes you into the Old West. At night, Disneyland often features dazzling fireworks displays. In electrical parades down Main Street, the floats are lit up with thousands of lights. Crowds also gather to hear rock and roll or jazz concerts.

Knott's Berry Farm started before Disneyland. Walter and Cordelia Knott opened a roadside stand to sell jams, jellies, pies, and other food. Soon, the lines were so long that they decided to give their customers something to do while they were waiting. So they built a replica of an 1848 ghost town, complete with a gold mine and a train ride.

Now, this amusement park has rides, shows, and other attractions. You can pan for gold, ride in a stagecoach, go on a log ride, see an ice skating show, or travel to prehistoric times when giant dinosaurs roamed the earth.

Magic Mountain is north of Los Angeles in Valencia. It is famous for its thrilling roller coasters and water slides. One of the best parts of this amusement park is Wizard's Village. Here, children can wander through the "punching bag" forest or the maze of tunnels in the "Swiss cheese." You

At Griffith Observatory and Planetarium, visitors can study the stars through one of the world's most powerful telescopes.

©Arthur Threadgill

The Los Angeles Zoo, found in Griffith Park, has over two thousand animals on 110 acres (44 ha).

can watch craftspeople make a variety of crafts. The biggest park in Los Angeles is Griffith Park. It covers 4,063 acres (1,644 ha) with hiking and horseback-riding trails, soccer fields, tennis courts, and picnic areas. This park is also the site of the Los Angeles Zoo, a transportation museum, a science museum, and a theater. At Griffith Observatory and planetarium, visitors can gaze at the stars.

Studio Tours

The people who run the movie and television studios know tourists are curious about how movies and television shows are made. Many open their studios for tours. At the network television studios, visitors can actually attend the tapings for a variety of television shows.

People who visit the studios for the National Broadcasting Company

Visitors can learn the secrets of special effects on the Universal Studios tour. Above is a scene from the display called "Star Trek Adventure."

(NBC) can see what a real, working, television studio is like. This is the only studio that takes people behind the scenes of television production. The tour guides explain how television shows are produced.

They can explain how the technicians create special effects. They may also show how—through the use of makeup—a young girl can be made to look like an old woman. Since this is a working studio, visitors sometimes catch a glimpse of stars such as Johnny Carson reporting for work.

At Universal Studios, a tram takes visitors through 420 acres (170 ha) of movie sets. On the sets, visitors can see how special effects are created for movies. They can experience a flood, an avalanche, and an earthquake. They can meet King Kong, the shark from the movie *Jaws,* a dragon, and aliens from outerspace. They can even watch stunt experts perform difficult feats.

As you can see, it is hard to be bored in Los Angeles. With so many attractions, it is a puzzle to decide just what to do first.

WORLD CITIES

What Makes Los Angeles Work

Los Angeles has been described as a super city. It is said that many cities will be like Los Angeles in the future. A city grows because it has what people need to live. It has jobs, transportation, communication, and government. It has natural resources, such as oil or good land. It also has ways for people to have fun. Los Angeles has all these things. For this reason, it has become an important world city. Each year, millions of people come here to visit, to live, to work, and to play.

Transportation

The freeway system joins all the neighborhoods of Los Angeles. It is important for people to get from one place to another. The first freeway, the Pasadena Freeway, opened on December 30, 1940. Now miles and miles of roadways allow motorists to crisscross Los Angeles to get to jobs and back home again.

Just as the freeways have helped the city, they have also caused problems. One such problem is the heavy smog that lingers over the city. To correct the problem, officials are now planning ways for people to get around without using cars.

Two new transportation systems are being built. One is a subway, or Metrorail. The first segment of the Metrorail will be in downtown Los Angeles. Other segments will be added in the future. A second plan is a light rail transit system. This system, which is also under construction, will be like a modern version of the old trolley system. Some of the rails will be on the street, and others will be elevated above the street. Sections of these systems may be ready to use early in the 1990s, but it will take years to complete them.

Communication

Newspapers, magazines, and radio and television stations also help keep a city running. It is important for people to know what is going on in their communities, in the nation, and around the world. Angelenos can choose from dozens of daily and weekly newspapers. Many people in Los Angeles read the *Los Angeles Times;* others read the *Herald Examiner.* People in Chinatown, Little Tokyo, and in the barrios of East Los Angeles can read newspapers published in Chinese, Japanese, or Spanish. Several magazines also focus on news and trends in Los Angeles. They are *L.A. Style, Los Angeles,* and *Valley.* Los Angeles has more than seventy-five radio stations. All the major television broadcasting companies have offices in Los Angeles. Many communities also have local cable television stations. People in these communities can tune in to see city countil meetings or other locally produced shows.

Education

About 195,000 students graduate every year from colleges and universities in Los Angeles. There are 154 colleges, universities, and specialty schools in the Los Angeles area. Some of these are state universities. Others are private colleges. Many are two-year community colleges. Still others provide special training in acting, art, music, fashion, or technical subjects. Some 200,000 people work as teachers or school officials.

©Arthur Threadgill

Many Los Angeles newsstands carry magazines printed in a variety of languages (left). The University of California, Los Angeles, is the state's largest school (opposite page).

In the entertainment industry, some people have unusual jobs. In the picture above, stuntmen perform a dangerous feat as part of a Universal Studios tour.

Working in Los Angeles

For a city to grow, people must have jobs. The millions of people in Los Angeles work at many different kinds of jobs. It takes many different kinds of workers to keep Los Angeles running.

Many people work in the entertainment industry. All types of entertainers find work in Los Angeles: actors, musicians, singers, comedians, clowns, and many more. But think of all the behind-the-scenes people. Set designers, stunt experts, writers, producers, camera people, and other workers are also important to this industry.

Another important industry in Los Angeles is the aerospace industry. This industry grew out of the city's role as a center for defense production during World War II. At that time, the city was producing aircraft, tanks, and other weapons. The city still leads in this area. However, after the war and during the 1950s, 1960s, and 1970s, interest turned toward space exploration, electronics, and the research connected with the two fields. Los Angeles now has more mathematicians, scientists, and engineers than any other city in the United States.

The oil industry has been going strong ever since Edward Laurence Doheny discovered the black gold in 1892. Since then, Angelenos have invented many methods of storing and transporting oil. They have also invented many ways to use oil.

Tourism continues to be an active industry throughout California and in Los Angeles in particular. The movie industry has been a major cause of tourism's growth. People in the tourist industry run hotels, motels, and restaurants. They also operate tourist attractions such as Disneyland, NBC Studios, and Mann's Chinese Theater.

Many people are also involved in construction work. New buildings are always going up in the ever-growing city. Office buildings, shopping centers, houses, and churches are all being built. However, construction work does not always mean new buildings. Many construction jobs involve the restoration of historic buildings.

Other people work in careers that are very similar to those in other cities. They are doctors, nurses, lawyers, and teachers. They are waiters, dishwashers, and grocery store checkers, cab drivers and bus drivers. It takes many kinds of people with many different talents and skills to make a city work.

Not everyone living in Los Angeles is a star. Most of the city's residents, such as these businesspeople, have more typical jobs and lives.

Culture in the City

People everywhere enjoy music and art. Every large city has a variety of cultural events for the people who live there. Los Angeles has many exciting museums. It has dozens of private art galleries. Dance groups perform ballet, jazz, and modern dance. Some groups hold poetry readings.

Some of the most historic and beautiful theaters in the country are here. Mann's Chinese Theater is one. You have already learned about the major theaters at Music Center and the Los Angeles Theatre Center. People can choose from a wide array of other theaters as well. Some are large and

The Capitol Records Tower was built to look like a stack of records. At one time, the beacon at its top flashed the word Hollywood *in Morse code.*

very famous, such as the Pantages on Hollywood Boulevard. Others are small and intimate and found in unexpected places.

Hundreds of recording studios and more than twenty record companies have their main offices here. Musicians who come to Los Angeles to make records often perform for audiences at concerts. You can hear all kinds of music in Los Angeles: classical, rock and roll, opera, blues, and jazz. You can hear a symphony or a punk rock band.

WORLD CITIES

The City in the World

Los Angeles is one of the great cities of the world. Important people from all over the world visit this city. Queen Elizabeth of Britain visited here. The late emperor of Japan, Hirohito, shook hands with Mickey Mouse when he toured Disneyland. The kings and queens of Sweden and Spain, the prime ministers of Hungary and Italy, and ambassadors from Iceland and Germany have all visited Los Angeles in the past few years. Former President Ronald Reagan owns a ranch in Santa Barbara (a city just north of Los Angeles) and has a house in the city.

The influence of Los Angeles is seen around the world. Levi jeans first became fashionable here. Now young people in England, France, Australia, and even Russia practically live in their jeans. Other fashion trends began in Los Angeles as well. These trends spread from Los Angeles because many people travel from the city to other places. Millions of people visit Los Angeles and take ideas home with them. Students from other countries come to study at the colleges and universities in Los Angeles. Movies also spread ideas about the city.

Movies are a particularly interesting way to spread Los Angeles's influence. Because of the movies, the sights of Los Angeles are familiar to the people of many countries. Movie stars and other entertainers are ambassadors for Los Angeles. They travel to foreign places and talk about their lives in Los Angeles.

Los Angeles International Airport, or LAX, is the largest of the area's five commercial airports. This airport handles an average of 150,000 passengers a day.

Los Angeles International Airport

The Los Angeles International Airport, or LAX, makes it easy for tourists and businesspeople to get to Los Angeles. More than one hundred airlines from around the world fly into this airport. Workers handle 750,000 tons of air cargo every year. This amount of cargo is equal to about 185,000 elephants.

The airport was built in 1928 on a field where crops had once grown. The first airport had one runway. Many runways, huge buildings, and hangars now make up this airport. A hangar is a big building where planes can be kept. A $700 million expansion readied the airport for the 1984 Olympics. Like the city of Los Angeles, LAX is always changing.

In a few hours, bankers or computer experts from Los Angeles can be in Japan, Australia, or South America. Tourists from around the world can fly into Los Angeles to visit Disneyland and see the other sights of Los Angeles. They see what America is like and take home American products. They learn about the American way of life and tell their friends back home.

Port of Los Angeles

Los Angeles is an important trading partner with other cities around the world because of its large port. The Port of Los Angeles is in San Pedro. Ships carry goods to and from other countries from this port. These ships come and go to Japan, Taiwan, Korea, Hong Kong, Australia, and other countries.

A Model City

Because Los Angeles is one of the biggest cities in the world, it is watched by many people. News reporters around the world cover what is happening in Los Angeles. People in other cities look to Los Angeles for ideas. They want to see how Los Angeles officials solve the problems of smog and traffic jams. They want to know how Los Angeles is preparing for the next earthquake. They watch to see how the city approaches a water shortage. Studying the problems of Los Angeles may teach people how to solve the problems of the future.

The City of Angels is a place to remember. You can learn much from

Los Angeles is more than surf and sun. As one of the world's largest cities, Los Angeles is also one of its leaders. What happens in Los Angeles affects people throughout the world.

its people and places. The successful businesses in Los Angeles, for example, are proof that Americans are a hardworking people. They are proud of their accomplishments. The many different people living in Los Angeles show that there are many different ways to look at things. The movies that are such an important part of the city give people a chance to daydream. Finally, the easy life-style of the beach reminds people that it is important to have fun in life.

Los Angeles: Historical Events

1769 An expedition of Spanish explorers enters the area that is now Los Angeles.

1781 Felipe de Neve, the Spanish governor of California, recruits eleven families from Mexico to settle Los Angeles.

1821 Mexico wins its independence from Spain.

1822 Los Angeles and all of California come under Mexican rule.

1825 Epidemics of cholera and smallpox kill more than six thousand Indians.

1842 Don Francisco Lopez discovers gold while digging up wild onions near his home in the San Fernando Valley.

1846 American soldiers march into Los Angeles and take control away from the Mexicans. In May, the United States declares war on the Mexicans.

1849 The famous gold rush occurs in San Francisco.

1850 California becomes a state.

1855, 1857 Major earthquakes hit Los Angeles.

1861 Heavy rains cause waist-deep floodwaters in Los Angeles.

1862- 1864 A severe drought strikes Los Angeles, causing great hardship to many.

1876 A railroad connects San Francisco and Los Angeles, contributing to the Great Boom, a dramatic increase in population in Los Angeles.

1887 The city of Los Angeles becomes more mobile with the arrival of the electric trolley.

1892 Huge pools of oil (referred to as "black gold") are discovered in Los Angeles.

1902 The Los Angeles Aqueduct is built in Owens Valley north of Los Angeles to carry water from the snow-covered mountains to the city.

1907 The motion-picture industry begins and flourishes in Los Angeles.

1916 The Hollywood Bowl opens.

1922 The "Hollywood" sign is built.

1928 Los Angeles International Airport is built on a field where crops had once grown. The one-runway airport grew into the present-day LAX.

1932 Los Angeles hosts the Olympic Games.

1933 A devastating earthquake hits Los Angeles causing $41 million in damage and killing 120 people.

1940 The Pasadena Freeway opens as the first freeway to join the neighborhoods of Los Angeles.

1942 A Japanese submarine surfaces near Santa Barbara and shoots at an oil plant.

1955 American film producer Walt Disney opens Disneyland.

1965 Civil rights riots plague South-Central Los Angeles for six days.

1971 An earthquake measuring 6.6 on the Richter scale hits Los Angeles.

1973 Thomas Bradley is elected the first black mayor of Los Angeles.

1984 Los Angeles hosts the Summer Olympic Games.

Los Angeles

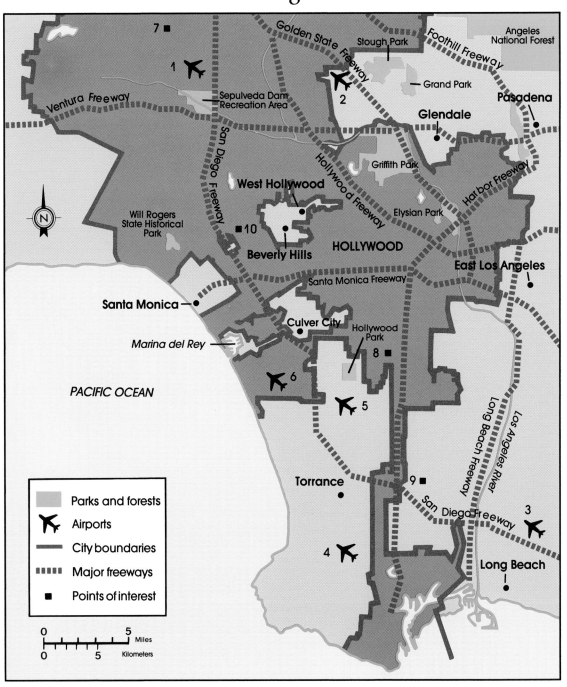

7 ■

Angeles
National Forest

Golden State Freeway

Stough Park

Foothill Freeway

1 ✈

Sepulveda Dam
Recreation Area

Grand Park

Pasadena

Ventura Freeway

2 ✈

Glendale

Griffith Park

West Hollywood

Hollywood Freeway

San Diego Freeway

Will Rogers
State Historical
Park

10 ■

Beverly Hills

Elysian Park

HOLLYWOOD

Harbor Freeway

East Los Angeles

Santa Monica — ●

Santa Monica Freeway

Culver City

Hollywood
Park

Marina del Rey —

8 ■

6 ✈

5 ✈

PACIFIC OCEAN

Torrance
●

9 ■

Long Beach Freeway

Los Angeles River

San Diego Freeway

3 ✈

4 ✈

Long Beach
●

Legend

▨	Parks and forests
✈	Airports
—	City boundaries
▪▪▪	Major freeways
■	Points of interest

0   5 Miles
0   5   Kilometers

Map Key

Los Angeles Almanac

Location: Latitude—34.0° north. Longitude—118.2° west.

Climate: Subtropical. Average January temperature —56°F (13°C). Average July temperature—72°F (22°C). Average annual precipitation—14 inches (35 cm).

Land Area: 464 sq. miles (1,202 sq. km).

Population: City proper—3,022,247 people (1982 census). Metropolitan area—7,477,503 people. World ranking—18. Population density—6,513 persons/sq. mile.

Major Airports: Los Angeles International Airport handles 32,722,500 passengers a year. Also within the Los Angeles area are Ontario International Airport and Long Beach Airport.

Colleges/Universities: 154 colleges, universities, and other institutions of higher learning, including University of California, Los Angeles; University of Southern California; Occidental College; Pepperdine University; Loyola Marymount University; California State University.

Medical Facilities: Hospitals—175+. Hospital beds—15,600. Doctors—6,900. Nurses—11,500.

Media: Newspapers—main newspapers are *Times* and *Herald-Examiner*. Radio—70+ stations. Television—13 stations.

Major Buildings: City Hall—27 stories, 453 feet (138 m). Bank of America Tower—52 stories, 699 feet (213 m). Wells Fargo Center—53 stories, 750 feet (229 m). Security Pacific National Bank—55 stories, 735 feet (224 m). First Interstate Bank—62 stories, 858 feet (261 m).

Ports: Port of Los Angeles and Port of Long Beach—81,869,000 tons/year total.

Interesting Fact: Los Angeles has the largest concentration of film and television studios and related production facilities in the nation.

Index